F J Wall (later Sir Frederick Wall),
Secretary of the Football Association
1894–1934.

THE
FOOTBALL INDUSTRY

JOHN HUTCHINSON

THE EARLY YEARS OF THE PROFESSIONAL GAME

FOOTBALL

REGISTERED
& PATENTED
Nº 17209

KING

RICHARD DREW PUBLISHING

To my wife, Carolyn

First published in Great Britain by Richard Drew Publishing Ltd
20 Park Circus, Glasgow G3 6BE

Copyright © 1982 John Hutchinson
ISBN 0 904002 81 0

Printed in Great Britain by
Butler & Tanner Ltd, Frome and London

ACKNOWLEDGMENTS AND PICTURE SOURCES

The author would like to thank Antony Kamm for his professional advice
and encouragement; BBC Hulton Picture Library for copyright
illustrations; National Library of Scotland, Edinburgh City Libraries
and the Mitchell Library, Glasgow, for supplying prints; and the Scottish
Football Association for permission to photograph material in their
possession.

Sources of illustrations are as follows. **The Book of Football**,
Amalgamated Press, London 1906 – nos 1, 2, 3, 19, 24, 26–32, 40, 41, 42,
61, 64, 67, 71, 92, 93, 95, 97, 98, 100, 104–111, 114, 115: A. Gibson *and*
R.W. Pickford (eds) **Association Football and the men who made it**,
Caxton, London (4 vols) 1905 – frontispiece, 37, 39, 44, 47, 48, 50, 65, 66,
101, 116, 117, 118: author's collection – 22, 23, 25, 38, 43, 45, 46, 52, 58,
59, 60, 62, 70, 74, 75, 76, 78, 79, 85–91 (from Dean of Guild, Edinburgh),
102, 103: **Scottish Football Annual** – (1896/7) 4, (1891/2) 5, (1893/4)
6, (1880/1) 10, (1899/1900) 34, (1893/4) 36, (1891/2) 80, (1887/8) 81,
(1894/5) 112, (1896/7) 113: BBC Hulton Picture Library – 17, 18, 21, 33,
54, 55, 63, 68, 69, 99: **Edinburgh Athletic Times** – (18 May 1896) 7,
(20 April 1896) 9, (25 May 1896) 73: **Illustrated London News** – (29
March 1902) 8, (12 April 1902) 84: **Athletic Journal** – (17 September
1889) 11, (20 September 1887) 15: **Quiz** (8 November 1893) 12: **The
Northerner and Athlete** 13: **Scottish Athletic Journal** – (29
November 1887) 35, (15 March 1887) 53, (26 January 1884) 72: **The
Scotsman** – (12 March 1887) 20, (5 and 19 September 1885) 51:
Molendinar Press – 56, 57: Mitchell Library 82: **Scots Pictorial** (12
April 1902) 83: Edinburgh City Libraries 94: **Scottish Sport**
(6 November 1888) 96.

CONTENTS

INTRODUCTION

W. CASSON Jr

FROM AMATEURS TO PROFESSIONALS

In 1880 the game of football was organised by a number of private amateur clubs whose members played for their own amusement on public grounds and in primitive conditions. By 1900, football was increasingly being dominated by professional clubs run as companies, playing on their own grounds and using paid players and officials who saw the game as a career.

In those same twenty years, the popularity of the game grew dramatically: 4 000 attended the FA Cup Final when Clapham Rovers beat Oxford University 1–0 in 1881, but a massive crowd of 110 820 saw Spurs draw with Sheffield United 2–2 in the FA Cup Final of 1901. The number of professional clubs in England had also risen from sixteen in 1885 to 65 in 1905, and their accounts show that professional football was by then big business.

What was it that caused this great change in the game in so short a time?

There is no simple answer. In these years many changes were taking place which affected the lives of large numbers of British people: changes like a reduction in working hours, the introduction of Saturday half holidays, an increase in the standard of living and the money in people's pockets, the rapid growth of towns and cities and cheap public transport to serve them.

Any one of these alone could not have succeeded in changing the local tradition of amateur football into the professional game; but when all the changes came together, the effect was dramatic.

Since that time, perhaps surprisingly, things have not changed much. The game today is very much what it was then. Many of what we think of as modern developments, like floodlighting and goal-kicking competitions, as well as the less attractive side of the game, like drink and violence on the terraces, have been around for a long time.

Leisure time for everyone

The growth in the popularity of football, particularly in the north and midlands of England and central Scotland, was only one way in which people's attitudes to leisure and recreation were changing. The process of this change can be roughly divided into four twenty-year periods.

Between about 1820 and 1840, the ancient sports and pastimes like bear-baiting, cock-fighting, ratting, bull running and village folk-football were either disappearing or being systematically destroyed. They were part of the old rural way of life which was being eroded as more and more people moved to work in factories in the towns. Many city dwellers saw these pastimes as irrelevant and brutal and tried to replace them with something more morally improving. It is surely no coincidence that the RSPCA (1824), the Temperance Movement (1829) and the Lord's Day Observance Society (1831) were all founded within ten years of each other.

As a result, between about 1840 and 1860 there was a sort of interlude when many of the older activities had gone, and nothing had come to replace them. Some writers of the time noted the damage this was causing: W S Jevons, an economist, for example, explained the situation very clearly in the *Contemporary Review* of 1878:

"If old amusements are by degrees to be suppressed, and no new ones originated, England must indeed be a dull England. Such it has in fact been for a length of time. Taking it on the average, England is as devoid of amusements as a country of such wealth can be. The people seem actually to have forgotten how to amuse themselves, so that when they do escape, by an excursion train from their depressing alleys, there is no provision of music, no harm-

less games, no other occupation for the vacant time. The unusual elevation of spirits which the fresh air occasions, vents itself in horseplay and senseless vulgarity; and in the absence of any counter-attraction, it is not surprising that the refreshment bar and the nearest tap-room are the chief objects of attention."

"Now I believe", he concluded, *"that this want of culture greatly arises from the fact that the amusements of the masses instead of being cultivated and multiplied and refined have been frowned upon and condemned, and been eventually suppressed by a dominant aristocracy. Amusement has been regarded as in itself almost sinful, and at the best as a necessary evil. Accordingly, villages and towns have grown up in the more populous parts of the Kingdom absolutely devoid of any provision whatever for recreation. It seems to be that the end of life is accomplished if there be bread and beef to eat, beer to drink, beds to sleep in, and chapels and churches to attend on Sundays. The idea that the mass of the people might have their refined, and yet popular amusements is only just dawning."*

His solution to the problem was to provide morally and intellectually improving activities like bandstands and cheap concerts; and although these were a far cry from football fields, the thinking of Jevons and others was a step in the right direction. Leisure, they said, did not necessarily mean idleness and vice. On the contrary, they saw a definite need to clear the gloom from life, particularly in the ever sprawling towns and cities, to encourage healthy recreation for all, and to support those new and worthwhile leisure activities which were developing.

So it was that 'games', which could be played in a relatively small area and in a short period of time, took the place of the old and time consuming country 'sports'.

In just over a decade, the Open Golf Championship began (1860); the first England cricket team visited Australia (1862); the Football Association was founded (1863); the first Amateur Athletic Championship was held in England

(1866); the Rugby Football Union was founded (1871); the County Cricket Championship was organised (1873); and lawn tennis was developed (1873).

Once the process had begun, its momentum continued. Between 1857 and 1898, fifteen different sports were nationally organised, as against three in the entire period till that date – horseracing (Jockey Club c. 1750); golf (the Royal and Ancient 1754); cricket (Marylebone Cricket Club 1787).

Here indeed is the key to the rapid development: it was not new games which were introduced (except lawn tennis) but rather existing activities, which had been played by a small number of people in a relatively haphazard way, which were developed and organised to make them suitable for the cities and the large numbers of people who lived in them.

The driving force behind this reorganisation came from the sons of professional and industrial men who owed their interest in games to the days they had spent at the newly reformed public schools, and to the philosophy of the rugged, games-playing, all-round man – Muscular Christianity.

"Life isn't all beer and skittles", said Thomas Hughes, Headmaster of Rugby School, *"but beer and skittles, or something better of the same sort must form a good part of every Englishman's education."* His book, *Tom Brown's Schooldays* (1857) had a lasting effect on generations of schoolboys and firmly established the importance of athleticism in the image of the true British gentleman.

His views were echoed by the Clarendon Commission of 1864, which emphasised that football fields were not merely places of exercise and amusement, but vital agents of character building; as a school song of the time put it:

"The rough and tumble, the dash and the skill,
The single aim, and the curbing of will,
Make men who can face good fortune and ill –
Sing hey! sing ho! for football."

But there was another side to the debate about the need to encourage the development of games for city dwellers. Frequent epidemics, high infant mortality and disease, particularly in the overcrowded parts of towns and cities, were worrying the authorities and leading to discussion on both public and personal hygiene.

From the 1840s, this had led to a series of measures to improve public health by providing baths, wash-houses, sewage disposal systems and adequate water supplies. But no matter how enormous the problems of getting such public works improved, they were slight compared with the problem of educating the general public in matters more personal. Sport was seen as a way of ensuring a fitter, healthier population, more resilient to disease. What was the point, asked C B Fry, the England footballer, cricketer and schoolteacher, of putting unhealthy people in the new, well-drained, well-lit, healthy houses?

Muscular Christians approached with missionary zeal the problem of converting these unhealthy people into a race of fit men of strong character, and took the game of football to the industrial workers of the north and midlands of England and central Scotland.

Not all the missionaries went as far as the Rev J F Jones of Wolverhampton who believed that *"St Paul was such an admirer of physical games that, were he alive now, he would exercise his diligence to complete his week's work by midday on Saturday in order to witness a football match"*; nor were they all churchmen, but the effect of their influence was the establishment of small, local amateur cricket, athletic and football clubs for artisans, clerks and tradesmen in the towns throughout the industrial areas, and the acceptance throughout society that some form of recreation, particularly outdoor recreation, was necessary for everyone.

In the early amateur days

Life in the early clubs was pretty haphazard. Where there was any income it was used to cover expenses and there was little or no attempt to encourage spectators. Indeed they were sometimes discouraged. Morpeth Harriers passed a resolution in 1886 *"that a board be placed near the gate warning the public that none except members are allowed in this field"*. This particular club had an annual expenditure in 1887 of £36.6.10, made up of ground rent (£7), police (15/-) – presumably for one important cup match, and train fares (£32.1.10). Even the early internationals worked off minimum budgets. At the England/Scotland international held on March 8, 1873 at the Surrey County Cricket Ground, Kennington Oval, by far the largest item of expenditure was the dinner given to the Scottish team.

Playing conditions were primitive: the *Edinburgh Athletic Times* in 1895 described matches 21 years before: *"Men came to the field dressed, their ordinary clothes on top of their football strip. On the finish of the game, the ordinary clothes were donned on top of the wet uncomfortable flannels, and in consequence, not a few fatal colds were contracted."*

Teams played at various times of the day. C W Alcock, describing football in Bolton in the very early 1870s, wrote, *"Practice took place in the evenings, and, in fact, the game was of a very primitive kind, followed after the hard work of the day had been completed."* Others played in the early morning. An advertisement in the *Leeds Mercury* of March 7, 1864 read *"FOOTBALL – Wanted a number of persons to form a football club for playing on Woodhouse Moor for a few days a week from 7 to 8 o'clock a.m. Apply K99 Mercury Office."* Eventually, this club played at 6.30 a.m., fined members 6d for being late and still attracted 60 on each side for their games. Membership increased to 580 and at 1/- per annum, and evening games were played as well.

This enthusiasm was infectious, and C W Alcock, the Secretary of the FA, wrote in 1878, *"What was ten or fifteen years ago the recreation of a few, has become the recreation of thousands."*

Early finishing and the Saturday half-holiday

During the 1860s and 1870s, more and more working men from an ever increasing range of occupations found that they had the time, the money and the opportunity to enjoy such games. Clerks, skilled workers, craftsmen, shop-keepers and small employers found that their standard of living was improving so much that a full six-day working week no longer seemed necessary. Although some clubs continued to play matches at night and in the early morning, it was the growth in demand for the Saturday half-holiday which was so important in the development of football as a spectator sport.

Early finishing on Saturday had been reducing hours of work since the 1840s, when some building workers achieved a 4 p.m. finish. In the 1850s, Edinburgh Trades Council had begun to agitate for a Saturday half-holiday; many textile workers gained a 2 p.m. finish, London masons stopped at four and skilled north east shipyard workers and Lancashire builders stopped at one. In Nottingham, many hosiery manufacturers were replacing fair and race week holidays with regular Saturday half-holidays in the 1860s, and lace workers achieved the same in the 1870s. Engineers were reported as working an extra half-hour a day to finish at one on Saturdays; others employed by Cubitt finished at four *"as the ordinary trade of London do";* and it was stated that the introduction of an early Saturday finish for potters and painters had reduced absenteeism on Mondays.

In addition, many of the more traditional craft trades were less rigid about hours of work and self-employed small shop-keepers and craftsmen could, if they wished, also take Saturday afternoon off. It was perhaps because of this freedom that such a large proportion of the early football players and organisers came from these occupations.

Sunday football never developed in Britain. The FA ruled (Rule 25) that *"matches shall not be played on Sundays within the jurisdiction of the Association"* and bowed to that peculiar child of Protestantism, the dull Sunday. Attention was firmly focused on Saturday, and, as the number of Saturday games grew, so the opportunities for both playing and watching the game increased.

So it was that the Saturday half day became a particularly well-known part of the British way of life and unique in Europe. Its appearance goes a long way to explain the influence of Britain in the development of new forms of leisure activities in the second half of the nineteenth century.

The rise in real wages

The reduction in hours of work went hand in hand with the rise in real wages. Without this, shorter working hours would not have been possible for any but the very highest paid manual workers, as it would have meant lower wages and a lower standard of living. The figure given for the percentage growth in real wages between 1860 and 1914 is overall about one or two per cent per annum. Although there were fluctuations due to regional variations, business cycles and the season of the year, the trend is clear: because of the decrease in food prices in the 1880s and 1890s, because of the growing power of the trades unions, home economic growth and the results of overseas investment, large numbers of people in Britain, particularly those in the areas traditionally dominated by the 'labour aristocracy' – coal, cotton, iron and steel, found themselves with more money to spend in their free time.

A G Markham, a journalist and trades union official, gave details of the way this money might be spent before a House of Lords Select Committee on Betting in 1901. *"You might put it roughly that the average earnings of a wage earner, taking into consideration the out-of-work and sickness and slack time would average about 30s a week* (the figure today is about £80); *he would give the wife 20s to 25s out of that 30s; the other 5s he would use as his private spending money and for his Oddfellows' or other Friendly Society's subscription. Out of that money he undoubtedly will amuse himself as he thinks fit, and will not brook interference from any person."*

A Child of the Cities

Football was not the only leisure time activity which grew in popularity at this time. It was perhaps the most spectacular and long-lasting in popularity, but there were others, still with us, like cricket, rugby and horse racing; and those no longer so popular like pedestrianism, professional cycling, baseball, and that other most sentimentalised entertainment, the music hall. They were all part of a new leisure industry catering not just for the privileged few as before, but for a wider market, and run not as a charitable institution or a philanthropic organisation, but as a business by commercially-minded entrepreneurs. And they all needed the larger towns and cities for their audience.

In 1881, 47 towns and cities in England and Wales had more than 50 000 inhabitants; by 1901 this had risen to 77. Football was an ideal game for the growing number of people within these cities. It was quick and exciting both to play and to watch. It required no special equipment (even a 'ball' could be made with rags or a tin can). It needed only a small field and could be played on rough ground by lots of people, simultaneously if necessary, without having to fall on the ground as in rugby. Rugby, its only winter rival, never became as popular because its administrators refused to allow knock-out competitions or leagues or to legalise professionals, other than in the break-away Northern Union. Football benefited from shrewd entrepreneurs and far-sighted administrators and prospered, firstly as a participant game and then also as a spectator sport. As a result, the enjoyment of a game of football became a regular part of the life-style of thousands of people every Saturday afternoon.

Getting to the Match

All of this could not be achieved without regular and cheap transport, both to draw even more spectators from the surrounding area into the city and to allow large numbers of spectators and players to travel quickly and easily between cities to guarantee a wide range of interesting and profitable match opposition. Most important in this was the railway.

Railway companies had been alive to the possibilities of excursions since the very beginning. Racing specials dated from the 1830s; the London and Southampton railway offered eight special trains on their newly opened Kingston line to the 1838 Derby. Thomas Cook had started his railway excursions in 1841, and the Great Exhibition in 1851 had seen the first major organisation of a system of cheap excursions for working people specifically for one event. Many seaside resorts had developed to cater for the railway day-trippers.

By the late 1870s railway companies had become aware of the opportunities of organising football specials to take large numbers of spectators to away matches. Newspapers began to carry advertisements and reports of such trains, and by the first years of the 1880s, they had become a well-established and well-patronised part of the football world. John McDowell of the SFA returned from an Easter tour of the Newcastle area in 1887 and commented, *"The enthusiasm in this district is very great, especially among the miners, who have been known to travel twenty miles to see a game."*

This distance of twenty or twenty-five miles formed a sort of maximum boundary for attracting spectators to the fixtures of big city teams in Newcastle and Sunderland, Liverpool, Manchester or Glasgow. Men looked at such a trip as a whole day out, spending perhaps 1/6 on the return train fare, 6d or 1/- to get into the match, something for food, beer and perhaps the music-hall, all of which would amount to three to five shillings for the day — a lot of money when the average wage was about 30/- per week.

Within the cities, it was the tram which made it possible for the football supporters to get around. Football clubs were careful to site their grounds as near as possible to a maximum number of tram-routes, or, if their grounds were on the outskirts of the city and beyond the housing developments, to use all their influence to get the tramway companies to build out towards them. At the Cake and Wine Banquet in

1887 to celebrate the opening of the new Ibrox ground of Rangers in Glasgow, Mr Dan Gillies spoke of his efforts to guarantee good transport connections for the spectators. *"He had called upon the Joint Line Railway Company, and endeavoured to make arrangements with them to run trains from St Enoch Station to Ibrox Park at one penny fares. The company could not see their way to run trains at such low fares, but promised to do so at three half-pence. This he thought was very generous of the company* (applause). *Again, the Vale of Clyde Tramway Company were building new cars, which they would run from Paisley Road Toll to Copeland Road. The company are going to lay a special line up Copeland Road to the park gates, and passengers would be run from the Toll to the park for the sum of one penny* (applause). *It was also the intention of the company to run brakes from the foot of Queen Street, the fares being twopence* (applause). *The Clutha Steamers would ply on the river for the convenience of passengers going to Ibrox Park. He was glad that such facilities had been secured for the speedy conveyance of footballers going to the new field."*

A patchwork of growth

All the developments that have been mentioned – the tradition of local amateur football, the extra leisure time and spending money of a growing number of people, particularly in the cities, and the expansion of the transport network – were necessary to the growth of the type of football which depended on the income from spectators, sometimes called gate-money football. Where they were all found together it grew rapidly; where any were missing, the growth was delayed, and in some cases, never happened. In the Clyde area, in Lancashire and the English midlands, all these elements were present, and gate-money football developed long before professionalism was legalised.

But other areas, like Yorkshire, south Wales, and to a lesser extent Edinburgh and the north east of England, had rugby traditions fostered by public school old boys. The same north east, London, and the urban south, had few local amateur works teams, as had developed in Lancashire and the English midlands in the early 1870s, nor had they the benefit of the missionary work done by Queen's Park in the Scottish midlands. Country areas all over Britain did not enjoy the high standard of living or the density of population. So at first development was patchy, because of these specific local conditions.

But by the late 1890s, gate-money football, nurtured by the equally newly developing popular press, had spread and gained a firm grip not only in southern Scotland and northern England, but throughout the whole of urban Britain.

The spiral that led to the professional game

This gate-money football, however, did not have to be played by professionals, as the strong traditions of highly competitive amateur football in the north east of England showed.

However, by 1880, some of the clubs particularly in Lancashire and the English midlands began to broaden their appeal, and to draw spectators not just from the original works or chapel where the team had been founded, but from the entire town or suburb. People in an area began to identify with one particular team as 'their' team, and local rivalry grew.

As the pressure to win increased, so did the competition for the best local players. This in turn led to clubs paying the best players to come and play for them and, as the practice increased, so these small local clubs were forced along a road to professionalism. The best players would only play for the team that paid them most; the club could only pay its players if the income from the gate was good; the paying spectators would come in large enough numbers only if they knew they had a good chance of seeing a high quality match; high standards of football could only be guaranteed by using the best players.

This spiral rapidly advanced in the 1880s, so that the legislation of professionalism in England in 1885 and 1893 in Scotland, really only brought into the open what had been in practice for years. Nevertheless, it must always be remembered that a large majority of clubs stayed amateur and an even larger majority of the players. Professional clubs were few, and professional players within them even fewer. What the legislation of professionalism did, and this was further emphasised by the formation of the English (1888) and Scottish (1891) leagues, was not to turn everybody into professional footballers overnight, but rather to place an even greater emphasis on the need for spectators to pay the wage-bills which were now legitimate.

Guaranteed fixture lists and regular large attendances turned the job of club treasurer from one of handing out train fares on a Saturday to that of a full-time business executive. The steady, if varying weekly income, at least during the playing season, together with irregular returns in the cups and patrons' donations, needed to be handled with skill and caution if players were to be retained in the close season. Increasingly in the day-to-day administration of the clubs, the part-time committee-man was being replaced by the paid official.

So, by about 1900, football had been transformed from a haphazard collection of scratch amateur teams playing games whenever they could, to a highly complex network of about two hundred mutually dependent business organisations, supported by thousands of smaller amateur clubs, much as it is today. The professional clubs were, on the whole, limited liability companies, with many thousands of pounds invested in their grounds and facilities, a chairman and a board of directors, a salaried secretary/manager, with a paid staff of players, trainers and groundsmen, all playing together in a league and cup system which was efficiently administered at a national level.

More and more businessmen, lawyers and accountants were becoming involved in running football clubs, especially as limited liability became widespread and as the close season wage-bills, which they had to underwrite, became larger. They realised that more spectators regularly paying the higher entrance charges to the stands at weekly league matches was good for business, and they consciously set out to improve the public image of the game. Hospital cups and charity shields proliferated; local dignitaries were invited to become patrons and to kick off important matches and some clubs, like Rangers, even moved their grounds to a wealthier part of the city. Professional footballers themselves became slowly less disreputable in the eyes of many of the extreme amateur players and administrators, and the game itself became increasingly respectable in the eyes of society in general. It became popular at all social levels, and for hundreds of thousands of people, weekly attendance at the local football match became an important part of their way of life.

Local and national politicians soon saw the vote-catching potential of their connection with a popular and respectable local club or their presence at an important national event. As Lord Roseberry said at the presentation of medals at the English Cup Final of 1901, *"This is the second year running you have had a distinguished Cabinet Minister amongst you to preside over this sport. It is good for football, and it is not bad for the Cabinet Minister."*

CHAPTER ONE

BIG
BUSINESS

PAISLEY'S FOOTBALL EMPORIUM.

[1] As the game of football itself became more like an industry, so it in turn began to encourage the development of a cluster of other industries which were dependent on it. Sports clothing manufacturers and companies making tickets, pavilions and fences were, like the football factory here, employers of substantial numbers of men. As William Shillcock, a successful Birmingham football boot and ball manufacturer wrote in 1905, *"Don't let people talk of abolishing football, or this country will suffer industrially, as well as physically."*

[2] American machines were imported to rivet uppers to soles; and

[3] an English machine was patented to manufacture studs.

[1]

[2]

[3]

[4,5,6] Clubs placed regular orders also with a range of other firms: printers for tickets, membership cards, share certificates, letter-headings, notices of meetings and match posters; restauranteurs and caterers for entertaining visiting teams, club dinners and annual soirées and concerts; jewellers for cups, badges, trophies and presentations; insurance companies, both for the ground and the players; and builders and hardware merchants for the construction and maintenance of the ground.

Clubs also provided a large number of jobs, mostly casual, in addition to the regular playing and administrative staff. Throughout the year there were litter-pickers, grass cutters, washer-women and money-checkers needed and in winter, snow-shifters.

Much of this money, as well as a large proportion of the players' wages, was spent locally, as indeed was the money spent by the supporters on their way to and from the grounds. The value of this business was recognised in the prospectus to attract potential shareholders to the Heart of Midlothian 1905 Company. *"Many thousands are brought into the city through the medium of football and, as a consequence, shopkeepers benefit largely."*

[7] Local pubs also benefited, though the relationship between football and drink is not a simple one. It was the practice, as N L Jackson, by no means an abstainer himself, noted, for spectators *"to adjourn to the 'football pubs' to discuss the results of the latest match, or the prospect of the next one"*; and pubs like the Vale of Leven Spirit Vaults provided the necessary facilities, as well as paying currently famous players to serve

behind the bar.

Brewers and publicans were strongly represented on the boards of directors, but at the same time, clubs expected breweries to support them with donations and the purchase of shares. Equally, there was a strong body of opinion which believed that football kept men out of the pubs, and that more football would lead to less drunkenness. As the *Scottish Athletic Journal* noted in 1883, *"The working population must be amused – is it to be the football field, or the dram shop?"*

[7]

"I say. Bert. why don't you make your own cigarettes.?"

"Because. Jack, I can't make Ogden's 'Guinea-Gold'"

[8]

BOVRIL FOR ATHLETES

Provides the Maximum of Stimulative Nourishment with the Minimum Tax on the Digestive Organs.

SOME EXTRACTS FROM RECENT TESTIMONIALS.

"I believe strongly in its value as part of an athlete's training diet."—**Jas. Wilson**, Trainer, **St Bernards F.C.**

"I have no hesitation in saying that a good deal of our success is due to Bovril."—**Joe Newton**, Trainer, **Heart of Midlothian F.C.**

"I look upon it as one of the best preparations for training purposes I have ever come across."— **John Taylor**, Trainer, **Rangers F.C.**

"I should like to express my firm belief in the great benefits to be derived from a liberal use of Bovril while training, and I have every confidence in recommending it to athletes."—**Don. C. Sillars**, Captain, **Queen's Park F.C.**, 1892-93.

"From my experience its virtues are incomparable, and cannot be too highly estimated by those enduring severe physical and muscular exertion."—**John Henry Tyres**, Amateur Swimming Champion.

"For bathers a more sustaining article could not be taken; I am always glad to recommend Bovril to swimmers."—**A. G. MacDonald**, Bathmaster, **Warrender Private Baths.**

[9]

SPECIAL NOTICE TO FOOTBALL PLAYERS.

"One of the most remarkable properties of the Turkish Bath is its ability to destroy the sense of fatigue and exhaustion. The bath strengthens, it never weakens."—Mr. ERASMUS WILSON.

ONE OF THE SIGHTS OF GLASGOW.

THE ARGYLE BATHS and HAIR-DRESSING SALOONS,

366 ARGYLE STREET,
(A little West of the Caledonian Central Station.)

Four Thousand People Patronise this Establishment Weekly.

THE above sketch only shows the entrance to the different Bathing Apartments. The Premises occupy 8,100 Square Feet of Floorage, and is acknowledged to be the Largest, Cleanest, and Best Bathing Establishment in the City.

30 Warm Baths, ... 6d., 9d., and 1s. each.
Turkish or Vapour Baths, ... 2s. „

HOURS OF BUSINESS, from 7 a.m. to 9 p.m.   *One Trial Solicited.*
A. E. ASTON & Coy., *Proprietors.*

[10]

[8,9,10] Other organisations, particularly those providing facilities for men like this Glasgow baths and hairdressing saloon and cigarette manufacturers, used football to promote their businesses. Companies making products like Bovril which were used by players, regularly quoted appropriate testimonials in their advertisements.

[11]

GEARY PUTTING IN A LOW SHOT WHICH BEAT COX.
A DRAWING FROM AN INSTANTANEOUS PHOTOGRAPH.

[11] The railways also did very good business, especially as a result of the development of regular league football throughout the country, and a whole host of specialist sporting newspapers was begun to satisfy the growing demand for news and comment about the game. Some began to print illustrations of the more important games, like engravings made from photographs, which were easier and cheaper to reproduce than the photographs themselves.

BUSINESS

PLEASURE

[12]

[12,13,14] Others began to use football cartoons, often poking fun at their own readers, who were largely male and therefore appreciative of a slightly risqué drawing and caption.

[13]

"A Very Good Half Back."

The Bailie Cartoon Supplement. 21st Sept. 1892.

HE WOULD PLAY FOOTBALL.

[15] One of the very early football pools, published in the *Athletic Journal* in 1887. By then, these prize competitions, run by newspapers, had become popular, and on-course betting, with bookies shouting the odds before the match, a feature of many of the public school amateur games of the 1870s, had disappeared.

FOOTBALL PRIZES.

A PRIZE OF £2 10s.

will be given this week to the guesser of the correct scores in all the following Association matches, on the following coupon. Any number of coupons may be sent in, or, if more than one succeeds in giving the correct scores, the prize will be divided :—

GOALS.	GOALS.
Halliwell	Burnley ....
Sheffield Wednesday ..	Notts Rangers ....
Accrington ....:	Bootle ....

ANOTHER PRIZE OF £2 10s.

will also be given for the correct score in the following Rugby matches; goals and tries only to be given; no mention need be made of minor points. Same conditions as to number of coupons and winners of prizes as under the Association rules :—

Warrington...........	Aspull ....
Salford	Bradford.............
Runcorn	Rochdale Hornets ....

Coupons to be delivered by Saturday at noon to *Athletic Journal* Office, Barlow's Court, Market-street, Manchester.

Name....................................

Address.................................

[15]

[16] Occasionally the newspaper obituary columns were used to emphasise a notable defeat. This 'funeral card' was for Queen's Park following their 2–1 defeat by Blackburn Rovers in the Engish Cup Final of 1884.

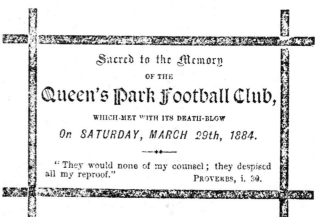

Sacred to the Memory
OF THE
Queen's Park Football Club,
WHICH MET WITH ITS DEATH-BLOW
On SATURDAY, MARCH 29th, 1884.

"They would none of my counsel; they despised all my reproof."   PROVERBS, i. 30.

[16]

CHAPTER TWO

THE
PLAYERS

[17]

[18]

[17] No one knows who were the first people to start kicking a round object about the streets. Some say it all began with a group of jubilant Anglo Saxons playing with a defeated Dane's head over a thousand years ago. Others point to the game of *calcio* played in medieval Italy by the aristocracy of Florence in a square filled with sand, just to make it more difficult. Certainly people were playing football in the streets of Britain by the Middle Ages. Edward II of England banned it as a public nuisance in 1314, as did Edward III in 1331. James I, II, III and IV of Scotland all in turn had it banned. The proclamation in 1481 linked it with another great public nuisance and read *"football and golfe be utterly cryed down and not to be used"* — apparently both also interfered with archery practice. Despite these and many more later laws, the traditional variety of folk football continued to be played in the street through the eighteenth century, as this engraving shows, and still survives today in Kirkwall, Jedburgh, Ashbourne and other places throughout Britain.

[18] England v Scotland at the Oval in 1878.

FOOTBALL MATCH,

WANDERERS, London, v. QUEEN'S PARK,

Played on Hampden Park, Mount Florida, Glasgow, on Saturday, 9th October, 1875

H. W. CHAMBERS,
Goal Keeper.

A. H. STRATFORD,
Back.

A. F. KINNAIRD,
Right Half-back
Blue and white cap

W. S. RAWSON
Left Half-back
Blue cap

J. TURNER,
Left Wing

W. D. GREIG,
Right Wing
Blue stockings.

R. L. GEAVES,
Centre
Red and white cap

C. W. ALCOCK,
Captain and Centre.
Cap—blue and white chequers.

H. S. OTTER,
Centre.
Pink cap

HUBERT HERON,
Left Wing
Grey stockings, and orange, violet, and black cap.

J. KENRICK,
Right Wing.
Cerise and French-grey cap

UMPIRE—ROBERT GARDINER, CLYDESDALE CLUB.
REFEREE—THOMAS HASWELL, 3RD L R.V CLUB
UMPIRE—W. C. MITCHELL, QUEEN'S PARK CLUB

HENRY M'NEILL,
Left Front
Orange and black stockings.

W. MACKINNON,
Centre Front
Red stockings.

JAMES B. WEIR,
Right Front.
Red and white stockings.

M. M'NEIL,
Left Back-up
Blue and white stockings.

C. HERRIOT,
Centre Back-up
Black and white cap—no stocking.

THOMAS LAWRIE,
Right Back-up.
White stockings.

JAS. PHILIPS,
Left Half-back
Red and black stockings.

CHAS. CAMPBELL,
Right Half-back
Red, white, and black stockings.

R. W. NEIL,
Left Back
Heather mixture stockings.

JOSEPH TAYLOR,
Captain and Right Back
Black and white stockings.

JOHN DICKSON,
Goal Keeper.

Colours : Wanderers, White Jersey — Queen's Park, Black and White Stripe.
Play will begin at 3.30 p.m. and end at 5 p.m.

PLEASE DO NOT STRAIN THE ROPES.

[19]

[20]

[21]

[19] The match-card of a game between Wanderers of London and Queens Park in Glasgow in 1875. Both teams travelled great distances in their missionary work to make the game more popular. Each player wore distinguishing cap or stockings, and each team brought its own umpire. They controlled the game, with the Referee being called in to arbitrate in disputes between umpires.

[20] The inevitable march to professionalism ended with its legalisation in England in 1885 and in Scotland in 1893. But professionalism had been a reality, even if illegal, for some years before that, as shown in this advert in *The Scotsman* of 12 March, 1887.

[21] A nostalgic look at a relaxed and confident world over a hundred years ago. The Harrow School football team of 1867. Boys from the school whose fathers were mill-owners, took the game home with them, formed teams with the mill-workers and so were partly responsible for the early popularity of the game, particularly in the Bolton area.

[22]

[23]

[24]

[22] Heart of Midlothian in 1876. In the 1870s, players wore long trousers, usually white and sometimes as knickerbockers, tucked in at the knee, a heavy wool jersey or open rowing vest, thick wool knee socks, often a coloured cowl and a variety of types of boots. Though

the laws of the game placed great emphasis on the types of studs or bars to be allowed on the soles of these boots, many players preferred ordinary shoes in dry weather.

[23] Heart of Midlothian players relaxing in 1878. The team soon settled on maroon and white as the club colours, but with a variety of permutations over the years. In 1878–9 it was *"Marone (sic) Jersey with Scarlet Heart, White Knickers, Navy Blue Hose"*: in 1879–80 *"Maroon Jersey, White Knickers, Navy Blue Hose"*: in 1886 *"Maroon and White halved Jersey with red Heart on white panel"*.

[24] By 1880, when this picture of Aston Villa was taken, the cowl had disappeared and knickerbockers had become the rule, worn first with knee-length and then with calf-length wool socks.

In 1884, Bolton Wanderers took the field wearing *"a loose white shirt with red spots"* which, it was said at the time, *"has the tendency to make the men appear much larger"*. They wore salmon pink in an FA Cup match on 9 January, 1884; their opponents, Notts County, were in chocolate and blue. Everton played at various times in their career in blue and white stripes, black with scarlet sash, salmon jerseys with blue knickers and ruby shirts with dark blue trimmings, before settling for royal blue. Such gaudy colours for a football strip, more like those in racing today, were common in the 1870s and '80s until clubs settled down to their present colours around 1890. Even the newspapers commented on the fashion parade on the field: Blackburn Rovers in their match against Sunderland in 1889 *"looked, in their pretty blue and white panelled jerseys, a very smart lot"*.

[25]

[26]

outside. Boots were of ankle length and light-weight. Jerseys were worn tied at the neck or buttoned like today's rugby shirts, with and without collars, and braces were sometimes used, threaded through holes cut in the jersey, which could then be tucked into the shorts. Goal-keepers wore ordinary club jerseys like the rest of the team.

There was a moment of madness after 1900, as shorts became shorter. The FA, alarmed at the discredit to the game, decreed in 1904 that shorts should cover the knee, but the edict was relaxed the next year to allow the knee once more to be exposed.

[26] For the professional, playing regularly for a club, a major injury could be a disaster. Clubs themselves stood to lose money if a star player was injured, so they hired physiotherapists and employed a club doctor (as this one at West Bromwich), to maintain a general level of fitness in the club and to attend to injuries as they occurred.

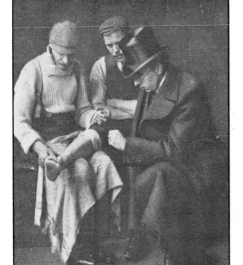

[25] Heart of Midlothian in 1899. By the 1890s, shorts reaching to the knees were popular, worn with knee-length socks and shin-pads (patented in 1874) strapped on the

[27]   [28]   [29]

[31]

[30]

[27–31] By the turn of the century training and capital investment in baths, gymnasiums and training equipment had become standard practice in all the major clubs. These pictures were taken at Aston Villa and West Bromwich Albion in 1905.

[32]

[33]

[32] West Bromwich Albion out for a training walk in 1905. The gentlemen amateurs of the early days of football of course never trained, and nor did the vast majority of amateur players, but by the 1880s, some teams were beginning to take their football and particularly the winning of their games very seriously. Blackburn Olympic were amongst the first to send the team off to a health hydro for a week to prepare for an important match – in this case the 1883 English Cup Final. Their training diet on that occasion was as follows:

6 am	Glass of port wine and two raw eggs followed by a walk along the sands
Breakfast	Porridge and haddock
Dinner	Two legs of mutton (one for each end of the table)
Tea	More porridge and a pint of milk each
Supper	Half a dozen oysters each.

It must have done them good. In the Final, they beat Old Etonians 2–1, and so became the first non-public school team ever to win the cup.

[33] Leeds City training in 1914.

[36]

[34] Specialists in football injuries soon began to advertise their expertise and Matlock House established itself as the footballers' hospital.

[35] No player, amateur or professional, wanted to be injured, and in particular, to lose income through their injury. So newspapers printed special insurance coupons, which also boosted their sales, and insurance companies advertised special policies for all kinds of sportsmen to ensure themselves against financial loss.

[36] By the 1890s attention was being given by equipment manufacturers to the prevention of injuries to football players of both codes.

[37]

[37] By the time that this photograph was taken of Bristol City in 1905, the professional footballer had become a respectable, smartly dressed and quite well-off member of society. But it had not always been so. The very earliest professionals in the early 1880s were paid illegally and thoroughly scorned by most of the amateur players and almost all the administrators in the game. But their numbers grew, so that when professionals were legalised in England in 1885 and Scotland in 1893, most of the bigger league teams at least were made up almost entirely of professional players. Their wages grew too. In 1888, even the very wealthiest of clubs like Bolton Wanderers was said to be paying its players an average of only 80/- per week. Celtic was paying its 'amateurs' the same that year! By the mid 1890s this had risen to about £3 plus a variety of bonuses for wins, draws and cup matches and Christmas tours.

Though payments varied tremendously between clubs and indeed between different players within clubs, it would seem that, in general, the average professional player by 1900 was earning, when all was included, about twice the wage of the average skilled worker at the time. Some invested their earnings and became businessmen. Others had businesses bought for them as a transfer incentive or when they retired. Pubs were particularly popular because as the *Athletic Journal* noted in 1890, *"A footballer behind the bar is as great an attraction as a long-legged giant or a fat woman."* Many, like Robert Crompton, the Blackburn Rovers and England captain and full-back, played as professional players but continued to follow their original trade. He was a plumber, and obviously a wealthy one because by 1905 he was driving to Blackburn's ground in his own motor car.

[38]

[38] But money was not everything. There were competitions to enter with rich prizes, here proudly displayed beside Isaac Begbie, captain of Heart of Midlothian in the 1890s, who won them in five-a-side tournaments.

There was, even at this stage, an undoubted sex appeal about professional players. Advertisers soon realised their potential, and the *Athletic Journal* noted about the Sunderland goalkeeper in 1890, *"Auld has the largest boot and shoe trade in Sunderland. The ladies like him to fit them on."*

Above all there was fame. Successful players and successful teams were fêted wherever they went. They travelled in special trains, were honoured at civic banquets, had boxes provided for them at music halls, and as C Edwardes, a sports commentator, wrote in 1892, *"They are better known than the local members of Parliament."*

[39]

[39] Howard Spencer, the Aston Villa captain, receiving the FA Cup from Lord Kinnaird, Chairman of the FA, at the Crystal Palace in 1905. Aston Villa beat Newcastle United 2–0.

[40]

[41]

[40] By 1909, the international matches were about the only occasions when amateurs and professionals played together in the same team. Status differences were still maintained – the amateurs in the England team were given their initials, the professionals not – but equality had advanced sufficiently to allow the team to travel together, to be captained by a professional, Robert Crompton from Blackburn Rovers (second from the right), and to be photographed together outside the St Enoch's Hotel in Glasgow in 1904.

[41] An international selection committee watching a trial game at Queen's Club.

[42]

[42] Once the grim ranks of selectors had done their work, the international match was an occasion for a great day out for the players, who might enjoy [43] a modest lunch on the way down, a quiet stroll before the game, and a slightly more exuberant party afterwards.

[44] Aston Villa v Newcastle United at the Crystal Palace, 1905.

MIDLAND & GLASGOW & SOUTH WESTERN RAILWAYS

FIRST and THIRD Class LUNCHEON and DINING CARRIAGES are attached to the 10.30 a.m. and 2.10 p.m. from ST. PANCRAS Station, and to the 10 a.m. and 1.30 p.m. from ST. ENOCH Station, Glasgow. For connections with Manchester (Victoria), Liverpool (Exchange), Bristol, and West of England, &c., see the Midland and Glasgow and South-Western Companies' Time Tables.

Scottish International Football Party.

GLASGOW TO LIVERPOOL.

MARCH 17th, 1899.

Menu of Luncheon, 2/6.

Mock Turtle

Fillet of Mackerel Portugaise

Roast Mutton

Cauliflower   -   Potatoes

Genoise Pralinée

Gelée au Vin

Cheese   -   Salad

Small Cup of Tea or Black Coffee with Luncheon or Dinner, 3d.

It is particularly requested that no money be paid without a Bill, and that any observations or complaints in reference to the service in the Dining Cars should be addressed to Mr. Towle, Midland Grand Hotel, St. Pancras, London, N.W., accompanied by the Bill which is presented for every payment made on the Cars.

Telegrams ordering accommodation at the following HOTELS will be sent free of charge on application to the Conductor of the Car:—

Midland Grand (ST. PANCRAS), N.W.   Adelphi, LIVERPOOL.
Midland, BRADFORD.   Queen's, LEEDS.
Midland, DERBY.   Midland, MORECAMBE.
St. Enoch's, GLASGOW.

HEYSHAM TOWER, near MORECAMBE (Terms en pension).

Passengers may join the Dining Cars at intermediate stations, and there is no charge beyond the sum payable for meals.

[43]

[44]

[45] It is impossible to compare the skills of players of different generations and to predict the results of imaginary matches between the best teams of each era. The players of one's youth always stand out as giants. Styles of play, however, did vary and develop over the years, with certain players being notable as innovators or as characterising the playing style of a particular period.

As captain and full-back of Heart of Midlothian, Nicholas John Ross was 'spotted' by Captain Sudell of Preston in 1883 and became one of the first Scottish professional imports who were joined together to make the North End team, the 'Invincibles of Proud Preston'. In 1888–9 they won the double, the FA Cup without having a goal scored against them, and the League (in its first year) without losing a match. They revolutionized the playing of the game by discussing and planning team tactics on a blackboard and by using chessmen on a billiard table, by their commitment to winning and by developing the passing game, using all players in combination and harmony rather than the 'kick and rush' or individual dribbling styles which had previously been used.

They reduced too, the level of physical contact between players, partly because, with the passing game, it was unnecessary, and partly because as professionals they did not want to lose money through injury. The writer in *Baily's Magazine* in 1891 noted, "*The professional or semi-professional player does not as a rule delight in hard-charging like the Eton schoolboys, but he well understands the way to bring down his man with an artful trip, while escaping the notice of the referee. A tricky style of play, which seems to have originated in Glasgow, and which is more dangerous to limb, if not life, than the*

[45]

old-fashioned straight forward violence has been making its way into the game."

[46]   [47]

[46] Bobby Walker has signed a coloured post-card showing all the International caps won playing for Scotland between 1896 and 1909.

[47] G O Smith the Corinthians and England centre forward in the 1890s. He had a frail physique but a remarkable control of the ball when passing and a deadly shot in front of goal. He played in the golden era of the amateur, for a team, the Corinthians, whose players were the cream of all the amateur public school footballers in England. Each year they played a charity match against the best professional team, latterly for the Dewar Shield. They beat Preston North End in their heyday in 1889, 5–0, Blackburn Rovers 8–1 in 1884 and 6–0 in 1885 and Bury 10–3 in 1904, amongst a number of other major victories.

[48] Stephen Bloomer, the Derby County and England inside-right of the early 1900s, like G O Smith a 'brainy' player with a frail physique and a deadly shot. He played at a time when the game had settled into a regular pattern of league and cup matches between entirely professional teams playing for large clubs and before large crowds. He

[48]

was typical of the player who did well out of the game, with a good income and a name famous throughout the land.

The Bailie Cartoon Supplement, 11th April 1900.

AT THE INTERNATIONAL

[49]

[50] Cup semi-final, Aston Villa v Everton, c. 1905. Photographs of the period in general show rather static games, often photographed from far off, with little of the intense running and athletic leaping of today. Such pictures, however, as also no. 44, do show close-ups of movement in the air and on the ground, and capture something of the atmosphere on the field.

[50]

CHAPTER THREE

THE
SUPPORTERS

Shiverers

ASSOCIATION FOOTBALL MATCHES.
1ST and 2D HIBERNIANS
Versus
1ST and 2D HEART OF MID-LOTHIAN.
At TYNECASTLE PARK, DALRY, TO-DAY (SATURDAY.)
Both Matches start at 4 o'clock prompt.
Admission SIXPENCE. *Ladies Free.* GRAND STAND, 6d. extra.
Members Tickets do not admit to Grand Stand for these Matches.
Cars from Register run close to Ground.

ASSOCIATION FOOTBALL MATCH.
DUMBARTON
v.
HEART of MID-LOTHIAN.
TO-DAY, SEPTEMBER 5th. Kick off at 4 o'clock prompt.
Admission Sixpence. *Ladies free.* Grand Stand Sixpence extra.
Cars from Register run close to Ground.

[51]

ROSEBERY CHARITY CUP TIE
Under the distinguished Patronage of the Lord Provost and Town Council of Edinburgh, and the Provost and Town Council of Leith.

HEARTS

KICK-OFF AT 3.30 P.M.
To be Played to a Finish.

VERSUS

Over £6000 has been allocated to Charitable Institutions throughout the City & District.

HIBS
CUP HOLDERS

TYNECASTLE PARK
GORGIE ROAD
On SATURDAY, 10th MAY 1913

[52]

[51] In the 1880s when clubs first began in earnest to attract spectators, matches were advertised in the weekly sporting papers like *Scottish Sport* or the *Northern Review* and also in local newspapers. Two or more games were played in one afternoon as an attraction and club secretaries were always careful to mention the convenience of transport arrangements and to encourage ladies, presumably to keep the male spectators under control.

[52] By 1913, particularly at a local derby match, there was no need for the other inducements to attend. A simple poster was enough to ensure a large crowd.

[53] Cheap transport for supporters in excursion trains was essential for the success of any home and away system of matches, particularly in the leagues; and for special occasions like the International, there was considerable competition between railway companies.

MARCH 15, 1887.]   SCOTTISH ATHLETIC JOURNAL.   31

CROSS-COUNTRY NOTES.

The Edinburgh Harriers ran from the Granton Hotel on Saturday, when the following members of the Cross-Country team put in an appearance :—W. M. Gabriel, R. C. Buist, A. M. Donaldson, D. C. MacMichael, W. M. Jack, J. Jack, S. Black, F. Lumley, S. L. Williams, and D. S. Duncan. No hares were sent out, but a very fast spin of fully nine miles was indulged in through Davidson's Mains nearly to Cramond, and home by the Ferry Road and Craigleith. A run in from Cramond resulted in favour of Buist, Gabriel and Donaldson coming next a long way in front of the others. The time of the run was 65mins. The roads were in very favourable order despite the snow-storm.

The West of Scotland Harriers' run on Saturday was from Cathcart. The ground, being covered with snow as it was, caused some doubt to exist amongst members as to whether the run would be brought off or not. About a dozen members, however, turned up at Cathcart and, after some hesitation, stripped to have a quiet run for a few miles. Owing to the snow, which, of course, made the going very treacherous, and looking to the fact that the championship is on Saturday, it would have been suicidal to have attempted anything like a racing run, as some of the team might have come off with sprained ankles or something worse. It was very unfortunate for the West team that the weather changed as it did ; they all need as much training as they can get for Saturday last, and a good fast spin on Saturday last would have done them good.

The half-yearly general meeting of the West of Scotland Harriers will be held on Monday the 28th curt. in the Langham Hotel. I understand that the closing run of the club has been postponed for a week, as several prominent members, who it is desirable should be there, cannot get away on the 26th. Particulars will be given next week.
TRAVIATOR.

GLASGOW & SOUTH-WESTERN RAILWAY.

FOOTBALL MATCH,

"ENGLAND V, SCOTLAND."

CHEAP EXCURSION

TO

BLACKBURN

ON FRIDAY, 18TH MARCH.

RETURN FARES	Pullman Train. p.m.	FROM	
		1ST CLASS.	3RD CLASS.
GLASGOW, St Enoch,	9.15		
PAISLEY, Gilmour Street,	8.17		
GREENOCK, Princes Pr.,	7.40	16/	8/
JOHNSTONE,	8.25		
AYR,	9.15		
KILMARNOCK,	9.55		

Passengers return on SUNDAY, 20th March, by Train leaving BLACKBURN at 1.52 a.m. (Saturday Midnight).

Through Carriages are run to and from ST. ENOCH and BLACK-BURN.

JOHN MORTON, Secretary and General Manager.
Glasgow, March, 1887.

[53]

NORTH BRITISH RAILWAY.

INTERNATIONAL
FOOTBALL MATCH

AT

BLACKBURN,

On SATURDAY, 19th MARCH.

On FRIDAY, 18th MARCH,

CHEAP EXCURSION TICKETS will be issued to BLACKBURN, from GLASGOW (Queen Street High-Level Station), at 8 p.m., and from EDINBURGH (Waverley Station) at 9.20 p.m. Returning from Blackburn at 1.52 a.m. on SUNDAY, 20th March.

	1ST CLASS.	3RD CLASS.
CHEAP RETURN FARES	16/	8/

Cheap Tickets will also be issued from SELKIRK, GALASHIELS, MELROSE, and HAWICK. For Particulars see Placards.
J. WALKER, General Manager.
Edinburgh, March, 1887.

CALEDONIAN RAILWAY.

INTERNATIONAL
FOOTBALL MATCH

AT

BLACKBURN,

On SATURDAY, 19th MARCH.

On FRIDAY, 18th MARCH,

A CHEAP EXCURSION will leave GLASGOW (Central Station) at 10.5 p.m., and EDINBURGH (Princes Street Station) at 10.10 p.m., for BLACKBURN. Returning at 1.25 a.m. on SUNDAY MORNING, 20th instant.

CHEAP RETURN FARES

	1ST CLASS.	3RD CLASS.
FROM GLASGOW OR EDINBURGH	16/	8/

JAMES THOMPSON, General Manager.
Glasgow, March, 1887.

[54] Brakes on their way to the Crystal Palace for the English Cup Final of 1906 between Everton and Newcastle United which Everton won 1–0. One of the most popular and certainly the most noisy and sociable way to get to a local match of a Saturday was with a brake club. By the 1890s, most of the major teams had groups of supporters living in the same area who paid a weekly subscription to hire a brake, usually a 24-seater four-in-hand wagonette, which was hung with banners and portraits of the favourite players of the time.

[54]

[55] Brakes provided for spectators by the newspaper *Pearson's Weekly* for the English Cup Final of 1912, again at the Crystal Palace. Barnsley drew with West Bromwich Albion 0–0, then won the replay 1–0.

[55]

[56] The Partick Thistle brake ready to move off and the banner, with [57] a portrait of Alan Raisbeck their captain, made in 1911 and still in the possession of the club.

[57]

[56]

[58]

[59]

[58 and 59] Brake clubs usually developed a vigorous social life with concerts, summer outings, Christmas reunions and annual general meetings, and there were joint club gatherings. Here two brake clubs are on a summer outing. The first group are in the brake used to carry the victorious Heart of Midlothian team from Waverley Station in Edinburgh after their 1901 Scottish Cup win; and the second, members of Hearts' Southside Brake Club, are at Roslin, a village to the south of Edinburgh, and popular for summer trips. They are in the brake which ran to Tynecastle from Causewayside via the Bridges and Princes Street, carrying at the time a club banner with the portraits of 'Cocky' Taylor and Davie Baird, both popular Hearts players.

[60] A ground plan for the second 1902 International between Scotland and England (the first ended in the Ibrox Disaster, see page 70) shows clearly the prices being charged at Villa Park for this special match. The markings on the pitch are those used from 1895 to 1905.

VILLA PARK AND THE ARRANGEMENTS FOR THE INTERNATIONAL.

[60]

[61]

[61] A football crowd crossing Trent Bridge, near Notts County's ground, about 1905. *The Glasgow Observer and Catholic Herald* described the crowd heading for Celtic Park for the Scotland/England International of 1898: "*From noon an unbroken procession of vehicles followed, the types ranging through the whole gamut of conveyances, from the snorting, crowd-dispersing motor-car to the harmless, necessary growler, lumbering char-a-bancs, ancient 'Buses', festive four-in-hands, decayed broughams, resurrected shays, natty hansoms, and flag-bedizened brakes moved and mixed in the tortuous vehicular current, the whole forming a pageant that only Epsom roads on Derby Day could equal. At Celtic Park – the Mecca of this caravan of football pilgrims – the scene was stupendous – imposing. An army of police (200) and soldiers (100+) marshalled and distributed the crowd. Strong railings, stout fences and impassable barriers kept the enormous masses fairly stationary*". Later in the article the Scottish team (who lost 3–1) were described as "*a useless, feckless jumble of Colossal Frosts. Slow, turgid, nervous, blundering, they made an awful mess of their mission and their name*".

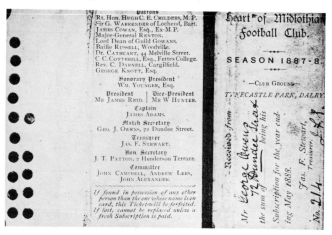

[62]

[62] A Heart of Midlothian member's season ticket for 1887–8 with holes punched down the left hand side each time it was used.

[63]

[63] Everton supporters with club umbrella, corn-craik rattle, flowers, and a slip-on cover to one bowler hat which reads *"Play up Everton"*. Local tradesmen look forward eagerly to the annual invasion from the north. As one Crystal Palace official commented in 1905, *"There are no people in the world like the Northerners. It is so much better for us when there are two provincial clubs in the final, as the Southern spectator only comes to see the football, and not to spend his money. For 'Geordie' of Newcastle, or wherever he may hail from, does not stint himself when he comes for the Final."*

[64] Newcastle United supporter at the Crystal Palace for the English Cup Final of 1905 against Aston Villa. His team lost 2–0. There were lady supporters there too, not to be outdone, organised into the Newcastle Ladies' Final Outing Club. As an obviously male writer of the time commented with incredulity, *"They had their own lady secretary, paid their own subscriptions, and with the latter-day independence of the sex, came to London in their own saloon without the assistance or company of a single mere male."*

[65]

[65] Cup-tie crowd at Derby about 1906.

[64]

[66]

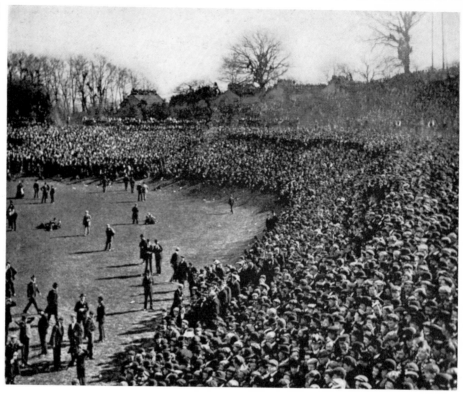

[66] The massive crowd at the Crystal Palace to see the English Cup Final of 1901 between Sheffield United and Tottenham Hotspur, the first south of England clubs to get so far. It is estimated that over 110 000 people saw the game which was a 2–2 draw. Spurs won the replay 3–1.

For this crowd, the largest ever to have attended a football match at the time, the caterers provided –
120 000 slices of bread and butter: 4 000 loaves: 21 000 rolls: 55 120 portions of cake: 1 000 sponge cakes: 1 000 pieces of shortbread: 20 000 French pastries: 10 000 Bath Buns: 10 000 plain buns: 24 000 scones: 6 000 pork pies: 2 000 smoked sausages: 1 728 gallons of milk: 200 rumps of beef: 250 chines of mutton: 150 best ends of mutton: 60 ribs of beef: 40 whole lambs: 300 quarters of whitebait: 500 lbs of soles: 22 400 lbs of potatoes: 2 000 cabbages and cauliflowers: 400 fowls: 200 ducks: 120 000 bottles of mineral water: and tea, coffee, sugar and alcohol, together with a vast army of people to transport it all, set it up and clear away.

[67] Crowd trouble at Perry Barr, 1888. Football, from the Middle Ages, had always had a reputation for lawlessness. The public school teams had gone some way to taming this, but riots, spectator violence and crowd invasions were relatively common, especially in the 1880s, as rivalry between the newly developed local teams intensified. Many invasions occurred in crucial matches, particularly in the cup or in derby matches. So well-timed were some of them that it is difficult to believe that they were spontaneous, but rather

engineered deliberately to have a good draw replayed for the sake of the gate money or because the local team was losing. By the 1890s, crowd invasions were less common, more the result of overcrowding as the popularity of the game increased and as clubs became more experienced in crowd control. Railings, turnstiles, fences and crush barriers became an accepted and necessary part of a football ground.

The only real riot took place on Black Saturday at Hampden in 1909 at the end of the Scottish Cup Final between Rangers and Celtic. Confusion arose as to whether extra time was to be played, and when the players left the field, about six thousand spectators tore up goalposts, fences, turnstiles and payboxes, set fire to them and danced around them in the middle of the pitch. Police, firemen and ambulancemen were stoned, fire-engines damaged and hoses slashed. The police, after throwing the stones back at the rioters, finally cleared the ground at seven o'clock, at a cost of fifty-four constables injured and the destruction of virtually every streetlamp around Hampden.

The crowd invasion illustrated here was the result of overcrowding; the clash between the two 'super-teams' Aston Villa and Preston North End in 1888, resulted in the headline *"Military called out"*. What really happened was that the ground was too full and too few policemen had been ordered, so at half-time, two soldiers in uniform who happened to be in the ground (soldiers in uniform were usually admitted free) were mounted on to cab horses and brought on to the field.

[68]

[68] A smaller crowd watches Spurs play Clapton Orient in 1912.

[69] Late-comers using every available vantage point to see Spurs against Chelsea at Stamford Bridge in 1913.

[69]

[70] A supporter's favour in the bright red colours of Middlesbrough Ironopolis in the 1890s.

[70]

[71]

[71] The start of the English Cup Final of 1893 at Fallowfield in Manchester was held up for some time because the huge crowd of 45 000 had spilled over and on to the pitch. When the game started, part of the crowd again broke through the barriers, while others pelted them with turf and clinker. Eventually to game was played to a conclusion with Wolves beating Everton 1–0.

[72] An afternoon at the football match was often followed by an evening at the music hall. As George Baird, a house-painter, remembered about his youth in Edinburgh in the first decade of this century, *"on returning from the Hearts home games at Tynecastle, it called for a quick tea and a short discussion on how Bobby Walker had played that afternoon, then off post-haste to the Empire. The 'seats' were hard boards without backs. It was always First House, and price for the Gallery was 3d."*

Professional football and the music hall were in some ways very similar. Both were newly created leisure industries and both catered for the same sort of people, as these advertisements for 1884 show. Both industries realised they were inter-dependent. The clubs borrowed the songs and the music halls borrowed the players. The currently popular song, *"The Man Who Broke the Bank at Monte Carlo"*, was sung by the crowd at the 1893 English Cup Final, and successful players were offered complimentary boxes, particularly after the Cup Final. Alec Leake of Aston Villa appeared on the stage of the Alhambra with the FA Cup before a cheering audience, after the victory over Newcastle United in 1905, and theatres used club loyalties to whip up enthusiasm in the audience. At the 1890 Christmas pantomime, 'Dick Whittington', at the Theatre Royal, Newcastle, girls appeared on the stage wearing the colours of various football clubs in the area and carrying their names on banners, which apparently caused great cheering and excitement.

"THE UNION LIVES"

Heart of Midlothian Football Club
ANNUAL

Amateur Athletic Sports
(Under Rules of S.A.A.U. and S.C.U.)

will be held in

TYNECASTLE PARK, Dalry, Edinburgh
ON
SATURDAY, 6th JUNE 1896.

Handicapper—Mr W. M. LAPSLEY.

EVENTS.	Value of Prizes.		
	1st	2nd	3rd
1. 100 Yards Handicap (on Grass)	80s	42s	26s
2. 440 Yards Handicap	70s	40s	20s
3. One Mile Handicap	70s	40s	20s
4. Davidson's Trophy, Three Miles, Open to Club Teams of Four (see Trophy Rules)	Special Prizes		
5. Half-Mile Bicycle Handicap, Class A	80s	50s	20s
6. One Mile Bicycle Handicap, Class A	63s	40s	20s
7. One Mile Bicycle Handicap, Class B	80s	50s	20s
8. Three Miles Scratch Race, Class B	100s	60s	40s
9. One Mile Novice Bicycle Handicap	40s	20s	15s

Entry Fee for Single Event, 1s., and for each subsequent Event, 6d. Entries close on 1st June with Mr E. C. STEWART, 16 St Enoch Square Glasgow ; Mr W. M. GORDON, 48 Castle Street ; Mr W. M. SIMPSON, 122 George Street ; and Mr R. SMITH, 166 Raeburn Place, Edinburgh.

[73]

[73–76] Clubs also generated their own evening entertainment. Soirées, concerts and social evenings were a regular part of the winter programme of amateur days, with sports days and picnics in the summer. As the clubs grew more like businesses, this social side was taken over increasingly by the brake clubs.

DUMFRIES FOOTBALL CLUB.

GRAND EVENING CONCERT

Mechanics' Hall, Friday first, 10th March.

PROVOST GLOVER WILL PRESIDE.

Come and Hear the Cream of Local Talent.

Come and See Fayor's Liliputians in New Songs, &c.

Guid Freen's I've been requested
These twa, three lines tae write
Aboot the Dumfries Concert,
Which comes off on Friday night.
They've arranged a splendid programme
O' sangs baith rich and rare,
And for tae hear a guid thing
I advise ye tae be there.

The President o' the S.F.A.,
Frae Killie, will be doun,
Likewise will Provost Chicken
Be owre frae Maxwelltoun;
And lots o' ither gentlemen
Will certainly be there,
And our ain worthy Provost
Will occupy the chair.

Now, when the Concerts owre,
And the Presentation done
O' the S.C. Cup and Badges,
Which the Dumfries Club hae won,
The hall seats will be thrown aside,
And the band will start tae play,
And with rollicking, jollicking polkas
We'll dance till the break o' day.

By W. Wilson, Irish Street, Dumfries.

Come and give us a Bumper House.

Come and See the Southern Counties' Cup and Badges Presented.

Front Seats,	**2/;**	Second Seats,	**1/;**	Third Seats,	**6d.**

AN ASSEMBLY WILL FOLLOW.

Gentlemen, 1/; Ladies, 6d. Secure your Tickets for Dance
early, as a limited number will be sold.

COURIER & HERALD

[74]

HEART OF  MID-LOTHIAN

FOOT BALL CLUB

SECOND

ANNUAL CONCERT

TO BE HELD IN

ODDFELLOWS' HALL, FORREST ROAD,

On FRIDAY Evening, 5th March 1880.

BODY OF HALL, 1/-

No. _Secy

[75]

Heart of Midlothian

Football Club.

GRAND ANNUAL

Soiree and

MUSIC HALL,

GEORGE STREET.

Wednesday Evening

21st March 1900.

Doors open at 7.   Commence 7.30.

Concert.

Reserved Seats, 1s. 6d.

G. R., Sey.

[76]

SOME JOTTINGS FROM THE INTERNATIONAL.

CHAPTER FOUR

THE GROUNDS

DEANE & Co.'s

FOOTBALL PAVILIONS.

DEANE & Co. erect Football Pavilions of various designs and any size. The prices given include Erecting complete within fifteen miles of London Bridge.

RUSTIC SPAN ROOF.

16ft. by 6ft. 6in.,
£21 5s.
20ft. by 7ft.,
£23 5s.
25ft. by 8ft.,
£28 10s.
30ft. by 9ft.,
£31 10s.
40ft. by 10ft.,
£38 10s.

PLAIN SLOPING ROOF.

12ft. by 6ft.,
£12 10s.
16ft. by 6ft. 6in.,
£17 10s.
20ft. by 7ft.,
£19 15s.
25ft. by 8ft.,
£21 15s.
30ft. by 9ft., £24 5s.
40ft. by 10ft., £30.

The 12ft. by 6ft. has one dressing room ; all others have two.

[78] The football grounds of the early 1880s were primitive affairs: a field, with a hut, a tent, or quite often a room in the local pub to change in. The Sunderland club received much-needed revenue by letting their field for grazing at 30/- per quarter. This particular clubhouse possibly belonged to Renton, one the great Scottish teams of that period.

[78]

[79] By the end of the decade more and more facilities were created to encourage the ever-increasing numbers of spectators, to control them, and to get income from them. So the ground was roped in, duck-boards were put down, pay-boxes were erected and then uncovered grand-stands were built, like this one at Hearts' ground at Old Tynecastle about 1885.

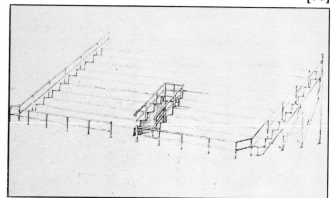

[79]

[80] Advertisements in the Scottish Football Annual for Braby & Co, one of the best known builders of football grounds in Scotland in the 1880s, after they had completed a new ground for Rangers at Ibrox in 1887.

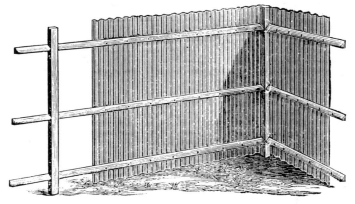

[81] Gradually the crowds and the grounds grew bigger and the technology of their construction became more complex. Wood and canvas stands gave way to concrete and steel; wooden terraces became great earth banks creating man-made amphitheatres. Most grounds were built cheaply and shoddily, and few thought of using them for anything else but football and the occasional athletics or cycle meeting

[81]

[82]

[82] Celtic Park in 1898, showing the banked cycle track.

The Ibrox Park Disaster.

[83]

[83 and 84] Ibrox Park after the disaster during the 1902 International between Scotland and England. A section of the newly-enlarged wooden terracing collapsed and 26 spectators fell 40 feet to their deaths. Over 500 others were injured. This was the last time that such wooden terracing was allowed by law.

[84]

[85 and 86] Plans for the redevelopment of Hearts' ground at Tynecastle in 1888, with uncovered wooden stands, a pedestrian walk and a pavilion which was basically a large garden shed. The dramatic changes which took place in the construction of grounds from 1885 to 1905 can most clearly be seen by comparing them with the following plans held by the Dean of Guild in Edinburgh.

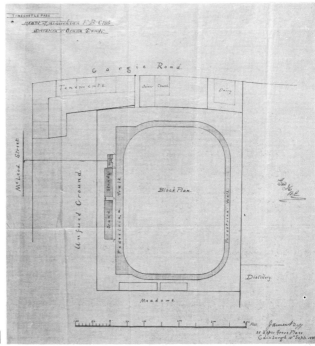

[85]

[86]

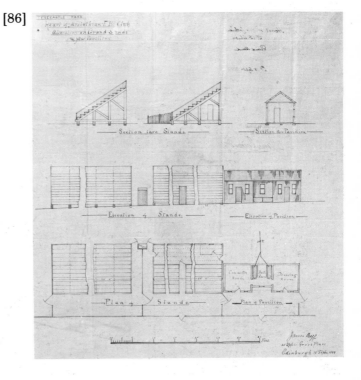

[87]

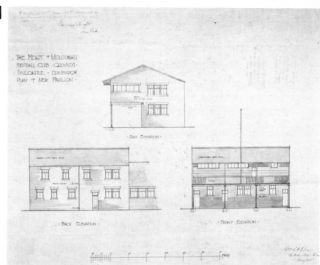

[88]

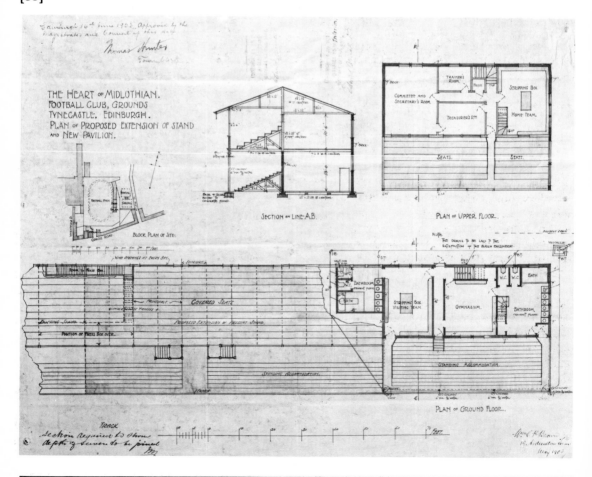

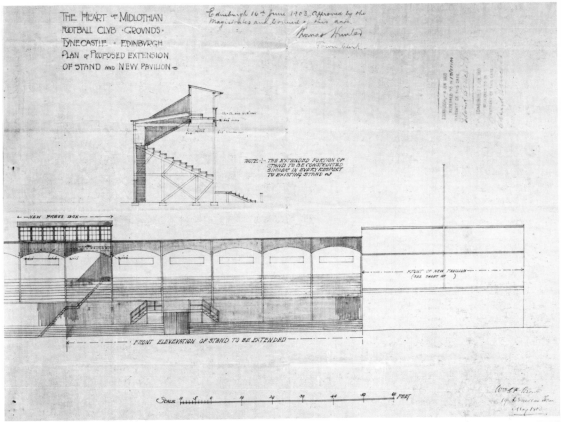

THE HEART OF MIDLOTHIAN
FOOTBALL CLUB · GROUNDS ·
TYNECASTLE · EDINBURGH
PLAN OF PROPOSED EXTENSION
OF STAND AND NEW PAVILION

[89]

[87–89] Set of plans for the re-development of the ground in 1903, with a large double-tier covered stand supported by iron pillars, harled brick changing rooms, gymnasium, committee rooms and a new press box.

[90] The stand as it was completed in 1903 with a banked cycle track. The turret at the far end of the stand was a press box. By this time football grounds looked very much as they did for the next fifty years – and as some still look today.

[90]

[91]

[92]

[91] The terracing over the main gates at Tynecastle under construction in 1914.

[92] In 1887, Sheffield Wednesday erected *"a massive iron railing"* around their pitch at Olive Grove which, it was said at the time, *"has the appearance of keeping the most excited, or perhaps, unruly audience from encroaching on forbidden ground"*. A similar iron fence at Southampton's ground, The Dell, during a match against Brighton on 3 September, 1898, has a very modern look about it. The six-yard rings, in which the goalkeeper could handle, can clearly be seen.

[93] The changing markings on the playing pitch. The only real changes in technology on the pitch have been goal nets, patented in 1890 by Dr Brodie of Liverpool; shin pads, patented in 1874, and worn outside the socks fastened with straps (see section on Players); the referee's whistle, probably first introduced at Nottingham Forest's ground in 1887; and the ball itself, which till the 1890s was made in segments like an orange, with button ends, and which became very heavy when wet. Goal-kicking competitions were won with kicks of only 44 yards and a number of players were killed while trying to head the ball.

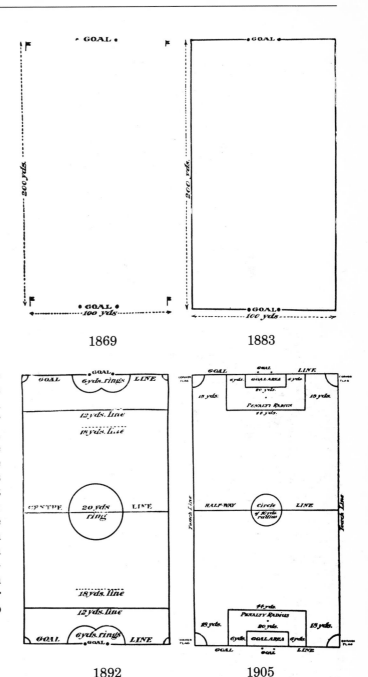

1869   1883

1892   1905

[93]

[94]

[95]

[94] The Glasgow Cup Final, Celtic against Rangers in 1894 or 1895, at Cathkin Park, home of Third Lanark. The stand is remarkably empty for such a match.

[95] Celtic, 1905, and behind the team a controversial stand. There were some attempts to increase the spectators' comforts and to improve their view of the game, but on the whole they were very few. Foot-warmers were provided for the ladies in the stands of a number of grounds, and in Glasgow an enterprising businessman and club director called James Grant financed the building of the stand at Celtic Park in return for a share of the profits. It was two storeys high, with padded tip-up seats and large sliding windows which could be closed when it rained. Unfortunately the building was inadequately ventilated and the windows had to be removed because they steamed up. The whole speculation was not a success and Grant lost a lot of money.

[96]

[96] The idea of floodlighting evening matches when many more people could see them had fascinated football entrepreneurs since the 1870s and a number of attempts were made throughout the country using different systems. At one match in Edinburgh a local reporter complained that he could not see the ball when it got in the shadow of one of the players; a problem, it was suggested, which could be solved by having a light at both ends of the ground.

[97]

Another experiment involved following the ball around with a spotlight; another, in Lancashire, had the ball painted white with two lamps on 30 to 40 feet high scaffolding; and in 1892 Celtic strung lights across the pitch at a height of 50 feet, but this too was a failure because the ball kept hitting the wires. Technology at the time could not produce a beam of light of sufficient power, and floodlight matches never became a regular commercial success.

[97] The Mayor of Southampton kicks off to open the Dell on 3 September 1898.

[98]

[99]

[100]

[98] Fulham's ground about 1905 and [99] the Crystal Palace during the English Cup Final in April 1911, when Bradford City and Newcastle United drew 0–0. Bradford won the replay 1–0. Both pictures show a number of soldiers in uniform, groups of ladies and the bowler hats and straw boaters of the obviously very respectable crowd. Notice too at the Cup Final the row of improvised stools and stands in the back row.

[100] The Crystal Palace during the England v Scotland International in 1905; and [101] the other side of the ground with its massive earth banking during the Cup Final between Spurs and Sheffield United in 1901. Picture 50 on page 56 also illustrates the enormous crowd which watched the match that day.

[101]

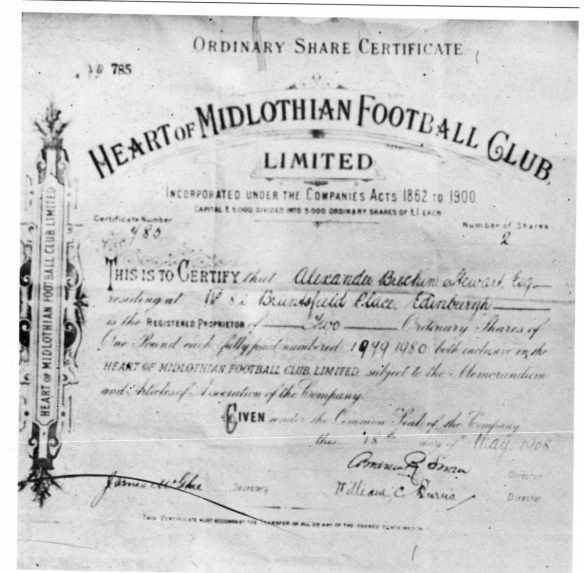

[102]

[102] A share certificate of the second (1905) limited liability company formed to run the Heart of Midlothian club. The first company, founded in 1903, went bankrupt.

CHAPTER FIVE

THE ADMINISTRATORS

[103] Between 1880 and the turn of the century, the finances of football clubs changed dramatically. In 1883, Heart of Midlothian, like many other developing clubs, ran an account at the local sports shop, Mackenzie's, which never amounted to more than £3.85.

[104] By 1904–5, clubs in both English and Scottish leagues (including Hearts) had incomes and expenses of many thousands of pounds and were being run as major business concerns. *"Next to being a City Alderman"*, the *Athletic Journal* commented in 1890, *"one of the most pleasurable things of this life must be to have a seat on the Board of the English Football Association or to be a member of some other leading Association body. There is no doubt that these big-wigs take full advantage of the various outings, feeds, etc, etc, perhaps, after all, it is but natural."*

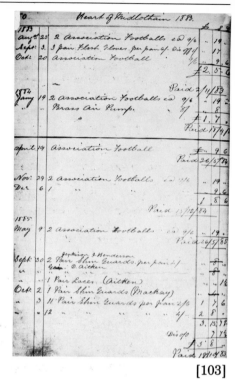

[103]

TABLE SHOWING PROFIT AND LOSS ACCOUNTS OF LEAGUE CLUBS FOR THE SEASON 1904-5.

NAME OF CLUB.	NET GATE.	SEASON TICKETS.	WAGES AND TRANSFERS.	TRAINING, TRAVELLING, AND HOTEL EXPENSES.	NET PROFIT OR LOSS.
	£ s. d.	£ s. d.	£ s. d.	£ s. d.	£ s. d.
Aston Villa	14,329 14 2	621 0 6	5,940 5 5	2,499 19 1	1,876 18 3 (p.)
Small Heath	7,209 3 1	559 8 0	4,438 3 6	820 7 9	949 9 6 (p.)
Wolverhampton Wanderers	5,450 15 4	380 2 0	3,617 17 1	844 6 5	119 6 8 (p.)
Newcastle United	17,065 0 5	715 10 6	5,118 9 2	*3,265 14 6	5,487 17 4 (p.)
Middlesborough	8,177 14 2	525 10 6	7,730 2 7	1,209 5 8	1,035 2 5 (l.)
Woolwich Arsenal	8,600 14 3	1,000 10 6	5,802 10 0	1,003 19 6	1,674 2 5½(p.)
Everton	14,053 14 4	333 17 0	3,748 9 7	1,780 15 7	5,108 17 7 (p.)
Sheffield United	8,074 13 1	362 9 6	4,039 12 2	570 4 11	†1,473 19 0 (p.)
Sheffield Wednesday	8,893 5 6	203 3 6	4,733 9 0	748 17 3	1,433 8 8 (l.)
Blackburn Rovers	5,743 2 0	380 4 0	5,174 5 0	964 11 9	1,542 13 10 (l.)
Bury	5,181 13 9	330 18 0	4,848 17 6	945 19 1	1,049 18 0 (l.)
Preston North End	6,957 13 11	131 15 0	4,345 17 0	895 9 10	917 5 0 (p.)
Derby County	4,410 17 10	745 1 3	3,998 1 3	930 3 7	1,467 4 7 (l.)
Notts Forest	5,504 0 0	750 0 0	4,645 0 0	455 0 0	545 0 0 (l.)

* Indicates police, gatekeepers, advertising, &c.　　　† Gross profit.

[104]

[105] The Committee Room and [106] the General Enquiry Office of the FA, about 1905. The Football Association, founded in 1863, was from the beginning the ruling body for the game in England. The Scottish, Welsh and Irish FA's were founded to govern their own countries in 1873, 1876 and 1880 respectively. Each FA ran its own Cup competition, and together they controlled the laws of the game. By the turn of the century, the FA was a highly organised bureaucracy of national importance, with its own offices in High Holborn in London.

[105]

[106]

[107]

[107] Some of the most important figures in the administration of football in England at an FA council meeting in 1905. At the table, far side, from the left: R P Gregson, from Lancashire, the official photographer for many of the international team photographs (nearest camera); D B Woodfall, also from Lancashire, Treasurer of the FA (fourth); F J Wall (later Sir Frederick), Secretary from 1894 to 1934 (fifth); J C Clegg came from Sheffield and was Chairman (sixth); C Crump had played for Wolverhampton and represented Birmingham District (seventh); J J Bentley, another Lancastrian, was President of the English Football League (tenth). Near side, from the left – W Pickford, co-author of a four-volume history of football in 1905, called *Association Football and the men who made it* (sixth); and William McGregor, an official of Aston Villa for many years and a founder of the Football League (ninth).

[108]

[109]

[108] F J Wall, the FA Secretary, at his desk in 1905.

[109] The League Management Committee, 1903–4. Though they had members in common, the Football League and the Football Association always kept their management separate.

[110]

[110] Major clubs like Everton had board rooms like those of large industrial concerns.

[111]

[111] The proud and successful officials of Tottenham Hotspur, photographed in 1901 with the English FA Cup. As football clubs became larger and more respectable, they began to attract more and more wealthy businessmen, full of local pride and determined to ensure the success of the local team. But for every board of directors of a successful team there were many more unsuccessful ones. As Gibson and Pickford noted in *Association Football and the men who made it*, written in 1905, "*Anyone who wants an experience that will turn some of his hairs grey, if not the lot, should obtain a seat on the board of one of the big League clubs . . . . While the gates keep up and the club wins a trophy or two, all goes well; but directly the team begins to lose and the gates drop, the director feels the fluctuations of public opinion like a thermometer notices the variations of the temperature.*"

[112] [113]

[112 and 113] Directors frequently used their position and their well-known footballing names to their own business and political advantage. Tom Vallance of Rangers and William Maley of Celtic are here advertising their respective businesses in the *Scottish Football Annual* of 1895–6. Others, however, abused it. In 1911, Lt Col T Gibson Poole, a self-made man, Mayor of Middlesbrough, President and Chairman of the Directors of Middlesbrough FC, was found guilty of bribery by a Special FA Commission, having offered £10 to Charlie Thomson, the captain, and £2 to each of the Sunderland team to lose the derby match which was to be played two days before the Parliamentary election for the Middlesbrough area, in which Poole was a candidate. Ironically, after all his efforts, Middlesbrough won 1–0, while he lost his election by 3 745 votes and was banned from football for life.

The Secretary

[114] As the finances and administration of the clubs grew, so did the duties in particular of the club secretary. The position changed from an entirely voluntary one, to one with an annual honorarium (gift for services) and then to a full-time salaried post. As the position changed, so did the secretary's status and his relationship with both the players and the directors. In the old amateur clubs, player, administrator and executive were almost always equals; but in the new professional companies of the 1890s, the players were increasingly paid wage labourers, the administrators were increasingly paid bureaucrats, and the executive were increasingly, though not wholly, wealthy financial backers, often autocratic self-made men, who made all the decisions and held all the purse-strings.

[114]

The Trainer

[115] By tradition, trainers were always photographed in their waistcoats, normally with sleeves rolled up, wearing a cap and often carrying a towel. It was they who were responsible for discipline, team training, rather like today's track-suited manager, but as many of them were paid less than most of the players, there was often friction, and trainers came and went very rapidly.

[115]

The Referee

[116] Originally each team brought along an umpire who controlled the play with the referee intervening only when the umpires could not resolve their differences. By the 1880s the referee had begun to take charge of the game itself with the umpires assuming the present day role of linesmen. Referees always wore ordinary daytime clothes even when on the pitch, normally a Norfolk jacket and knickerbockers, a collar, tie and a tweed cap.

Charles W Alcock

[117] Two men stood out as the most important figures in the government of football as it went through the difficult transition from a minority game to a major leisure industry, and the British national winter sport. As a member of the FA Committee from 1866, Alcock was one of the originators of the idea of the FA Cup, and was a captain of the Wanderers, who won the cup in 1872, 1873, 1876, 1877 and 1878. He was secretary of the FA from 1870 to 1895 and a member of the committee of the FA set up to consider the matter of professionalism, which by the early 1880s had become a major issue, as more and more Lancashire clubs in particular were importing Scottish players and paying them. Professionalism was strictly against the rules of the amateur-dominated FA and several clubs were expelled in 1884 for payments to players. As a result, a series of meetings took place in Bolton, Blackburn and Manchester to form a breakaway British Football Association. Alcock saw the potential damage to the overall structure of the game, and proposed, at a special general meeting of the FA in November 1884, that professionalism be legalised. The motion stirred up considerable

[116]

emotion and was rejected by an FA finely divided on the issue. It was rejected again in March, but on 20 July, 1885, in Anderton's Hotel in London at another special general meeting, professionalism, under stringent conditions, was made legal in England. Scotland, lacking the wisdom, foresight and tolerance of men like Alcock, had to wait till 1893.

Arthur Fitzgerald, Lord Kinnaird

[118] One of the 'Scotland' team in the first International in 1870, he went on to be a member of the Committee of the FA in 1868, Treasurer in 1877 and President from 1890 till his death in 1923. He was a merchant banker, a large landowner (Rossie Priory in Perthshire) and Lord High Commissioner to the Church of Scotland; but he is best remembered for his guiding influence in the early years of the game of football, and particularly when, in the early 1880s, it was threatened with irrevocable division over the question of professionalism. He saw football as a classless game, one which united people who were socially very different, and one which had a beneficial effect on society in general. *"I believe,"* he wrote, *"that all right-minded people have good reason to thank God for the great progress of this popular national game."*

[117]   [118]